Christmas

Gifts

2025

Lago Vista Writers Group

ecopy 8/2025 ISBN 13: 978-1-965535-20--2

paperback 8/2025 ISBN 13: 978-1-965535-21-9

For Information, address rseibert@advancedconceptdesign.com

axlerod@peoplepc.com

Printed in the United States of America

Contents

The Christmas Miracle of Maryland Street by JE Warr

Nestled in the pine-scented embrace of Cloudcroft, New Mexico—a tiny mountain haven where the air was crisp enough to snap your worries in half and the biggest drama was whether the elk would photobomb your picnic—lived the Warr family. We were the picture of small-town serenity: me, Jim Warr, a mild-mannered mutual fund salesman who moonlighted as a weekend woodworker (mostly because it gave me an excuse to buy power tools I barely knew how to use); my wife Vickie, a schoolteacher with a laugh like wind chimes and a knack for turning any leftover into a gourmet casserole; our son Casey, a gangly 10-year-old aspiring inventor whose latest creation was a

"self-watering plant pot" that somehow flooded the garage; and our daughter Julie, 14 going on 40, with her nose perpetually buried in a book and a sassy comeback for every occasion. Oh, and let's not forget Henry, our massive German Shepherd that for some unknown reason always smelled like tortillas and outweighed Casey by a good 20 pounds. He thought his job was to herd the family like wayward sheep, complete with judgmental stares when we strayed from the couch and vicious growls when we stepped over him while he was sleeping.

Life in Cloudcroft was paradise on easy mode. Mornings started with Vickie making biscuits that could wake the dead, Casey tinkering with gadgets that occasionally exploded (in a fun, non-lawsuit way), Julie reciting fun facts about dinosaurs or binary particles over breakfast, and Henry sprawled across the kitchen floor like a furry rug with a pulse waiting for his share of our breakfast. We'd gather around the table, sharing stories and laughs, the kind of family that made Hallmark movies look like gritty documentaries. But change was afoot—Vickie had landed a dream job as a department head at Cibola High School in Albuquerque, and I figured a city move might finally give my woodworking hobby some urban flair (or at least access to a Home Depot that wasn't a hour drive away). We were excited, buzzing like kids before Christmas, even though we were trading mountain vistas for strip malls and traffic. "It's an adventure!" Vickie declared, packing boxes with the enthusiasm of a general marshaling troops. Casey dreamed of city skate parks, Julie of libraries the size of small countries, and Henry... well, he just wagged his tail because we were stress free and happy.

Little did we know, our new slice of suburbia in Northeast Albuquerque on Maryland street came with a complimentary side of chaos, courtesy of the neighbor across from us. From the moving truck, we first spotted him: a large guy in his 50s, pacing his overgrown lawn in mismatched socks and a faded Albuquerque Isotopes cap, muttering to himself while watering a patch of dirt that hadn't seen a flower since the Reagan administration. There seemed to be dozens of broken

eggshells scattered everywhere. He looked harmless, even pitiable—like a lost soul who'd wandered out of a Tom Waits song. "Poor fella," Vickie whispered as we unloaded boxes. "Maybe he's just lonely. We should bake him cookies." Casey nodded solemnly. "Yeah, or I could build him a robot friend!" Julie rolled her eyes. "Dad, he looks like he argues with squirrels. Let's not." I chuckled, feeling a twinge of sympathy. Generations of kids in the neighborhood called him "Crazy Larry" or "The Maryland Man" (rumor had it he'd fled Alamosa after some unspecified "incident" involving a crab boil and a city councilman), but to us newcomers, he was just Eccentric. We felt sorry for him at first, figuring a little neighborly kindness could turn things around.

Boy, were we wrong. The terrorism kicked off our very first night, like a welcome wagon from hell. We'd collapsed into bed exhausted but giddy, the kids whispering about their new rooms, Vickie snuggling close with dreams of urban farmer's markets dancing in her head. Henry was out cold at the foot of the bed, his snores rumbling like a distant thunderstorm and Peewee our cat snuggling up next to him. Then, at 12:30 AM sharp, the apocalypse erupted: engines roaring like angry dragons, tires screeching in high-pitched wails, and a barrage of shouted cuss words that could've peeled the enamel off their teeth. It sounded like a demolition derby had crashed into our front yard, or maybe a gang of bikers reenacting Mad Max on a budget.

Vickie bolted upright, clutching the sheets like a lifeline. "Jim, what in the world?" Casey yelped from his room, "Is it zombies? I knew I should've packed my slingshot!" Julie, ever the pragmatist, shouted, "It's probably just fireworks... or a

murder!" Henry, our furry guardian, wasn't having any of it—he leaped up with a snarl that could've scared off Satan himself, his hackles raised like porcupine quills, his teeth looking like "The Predator", his barking deep and thunderous enough to

rattle the windows.

I fumbled out of bed, heart pounding, grabbing whatever clothes were closest (which turned out to be Vickie's floral robe— hey, desperate times). By the time I yanked on my boots and stumbled to the door, the noise had

5

vanished, leaving only the mocking chirp of crickets and a faint whiff of burnt rubber. Peeking out, the street was empty, bathed in the soft glow of streetlights. "False alarm?" I muttered, but deep down, I knew better.

The next morning brought the encore: our house and cars slathered in smashed eggs, yolks dripping like some abstract art installation had gone wrong. "What fresh nonsense is this?" I grumbled, hose in hand, scrubbing away the gooey mess. I've been known to ruffle feathers— back in Cloudcroft, I once accidentally mowed a neighbor's prize petunias during a heated debate over fence lines—but I swear on my power tools, I'd done zilch to deserve this Eggpocalypse'. As I worked, I noticed two neighbors across the way doing the same sad dance: a retired couple with matching visors, hosing down their siding while exchanging knowing glances. "New here?" the husband called over, his voice dripping with weary amusement. "Welcome to Larry's neighborhood watch. He does this every weekend. Last week, it was toilet paper; consider eggs an upgrade."

Vickie joined me outside, arms crossed, her teacherly patience already fraying. "Jim, that poor man. Casey, ever the optimist, piped up from the driveway, "Maybe it's a prank! I could rig a counter-trap with water balloons!" Julie smirked, book in hand. "Or we could just call

6

animal control—on Henry, to sic him on Larry."
Henry, sensing the drama, let out a low woof of
agreement, his tail thumping like he was ready
for round two.

As the day wore on, we pieced together the
legend of Crazy Larry from whispered
neighborhood lore. Turns out, he wasn't just
eccentric; he was a one-man symphony of
mayhem. He was some kind of mad scientist
who moved from Alamosa years ago, fleeing
what he called "the crab conspiracy" (don't ask),
and now spent his days revving old muscle cars
in his garage and yelling at passersby about
government cheese. We still felt a flicker of
pity—maybe he was just misunderstood, a
victim of bad luck and worse social skills. But
that night, when the engines revved again and a
fresh volley of profanities echoed, sympathy
started cracking like those eggshells. I grabbed a
flashlight and marched across the street, Henry at
my heel like a loyal enforcer. "Larry!" I called,
trying to sound neighborly. "We need to talk!"
He was hiding behind an evergreen tree in front
of our house between the sidewalk and the street.
I realized that when those teenagers drove by to
egg his house he would jump out from behind
my tree and ambush them by hitting their car
with a foot long multi battery flashlight. Thus,
they would also egg my house.

What followed was a standoff straight out of a Coen Brothers flick: Larry emerged from his shadows, eyes wild, clutching a flashlight like Excalibur. "You from the agency?" he snarled. "I knew it! The clouds told me!" I blinked. "Uh, no, just your new neighbor. About the eggs..." He

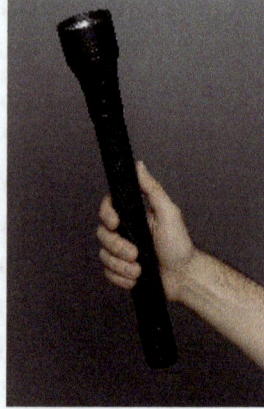

paused, then burst into laughter cackle that echoed down the block. "Eggs? That's my welcome gift! Protein for the apocalypse!" Vickie, watching from our porch, muttered, "Great, now we're dealing with a doomsday prepper who shops at the dairy aisle."

Vickie ask about Crazy Larry at school and all the kids knew about him. No one knows how it got started but for generations kids had made him the target of their vaporous revenge. They all recounted how they would drive by honking and doing burnouts to lure him out. He always obliged them and gave them a chance to through eggs at him.

Over the next weeks, Larry's antics escalated in hilariously horrifying ways: midnight drag races that left skid marks like abstract graffiti, random shouts about "the Maryland Mandate," and once, a flock of plastic flamingos mysteriously planted

8

in our yard overnight. But amid the chaos, our family bonded tighter—Casey invented a "Larry Alarm" (a motion-sensor light that lite

up our neighborhood like a Friday night high school foot game.), Julie documented it all in a "Neighborhood Nutjob Journal," and Vickie turned it into teachable moments about empathy (while plotting petty revenges like signing him up for junk mail). Even Henry got in on the fun, chasing Larry's cats with the enthusiasm of a puppy half his size.

In the end, Crazy Larry became less a terror and more a quirky fixture, like that uncle who shows up to holidays with conspiracy theories and bad jokes. We never fully tamed him—Albuquerque wasn't Cloudcroft, after all—but we learned to laugh through the lunacy. And hey, at least our eggs were always fresh and scrambled. Now I know why this house was underpriced.

Those kids were like the mailman, neither rain nor snow would keep them from their appointed rounds. When Casey said , "Let there be light" things change on our side of the street. Crazy Larry stayed away from that all reviling motion activated beacon, but hundreds of kids had made him into a monster that they could vanquish, and he freely participated by, excuse the pun, Egging them on. It takes two to tango.

The weeks rolled on, and Larry's chaos hit new heights of absurdity. One night, we woke to find our lawn dotted with plastic flamingos, their beady eyes glinting like they were mocking us. "They've escalated to lawn art terrorism!" I groaned, yanking them out while Casey suggested turning them into a flamingo-powered generator. Another time, Larry serenaded the street at 3 AM with a megaphone rant about "the Maryland Mandate," which, best we could tell, was his theory that the government was hiding alien recipes in fast-food ketchup packets. Vickie, sipping her coffee, muttered, "I'm one mandate away from signing him up for every spam list in America." But amid the madness, we found our rhythm: Casey's "Larry Alarm"—a motion-sensor floodlight that turned our yard into a Friday night football stadium—kept Larry from hiding behind our evergreen,

though it also scared the pizza guy half to death. Julie's journal became a neighborhood bestseller, passed around like contraband at block parties, and Henry's cat-chasing escapades gave Larry's strays a cardio workout they didn't sign up for. Then came Christmas Eve, when the street's simmering saga took a turn straight out of a holiday miracle flick. Enter Joey, a 16-year-old junior from Vickie's school, built like a

linebacker but with a heart softer than a marshmallow. A star on the football team, Joey was the kid who'd stop a game

to help a freshman tie his cleats, a devout Church of Christ regular who loved Jimsus, his parents, kids, and even the scruffiest alley cats. He was no bully—more like the guy who'd carry your groceries and pray for your soul in the same breath. That night, Joey was cruising the drag with his buddies in Steve's Oldsmobile Vista Cruiser, a station wagon so retro it probably had an 8-track player, with teammates Fred and Steve. Over Cokes at the corner store, Fred, the instigator with a grin like a used-car salesman, said, "Let's grab some eggs and give Crazy

Larry his Christmas omelet!" Joey laughed, figuring it was just another round of the neighborhood's favorite sport.

But Maryland Street had changed. The cops, fed up with Larry's midnight drag races and the kids' retaliatory egging's, had slapped barricades at one end, turning it into a dead-end trap. Steve, behind the wheel, rolled down the street, spotting Larry's silhouette lurking behind our evergreen tree like a low-budget ninja. Joey and Fred, each armed with six eggs, leaned out the windows, ready to lob their festive payload as Larry charged, twelve-inch flashlight raised like a caveman's club. The plan was simple: egg Larry, dodge the flashlight, peel out. But Joey's aim, fueled by adrenaline and maybe one too many Mountain Dews, went short. An egg splatted on the asphalt right in front of Larry, who slipped like a cartoon villain on a banana peel, careening into the Vista Cruiser with a sickening *kurthump*. His head smacked the windshield, and he crumpled to the street, motionless.

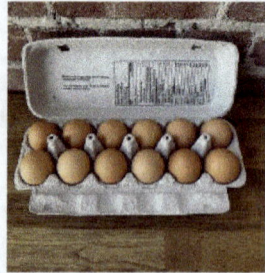

Panic erupted. Steve, eyes wide, floored it, tires squealing as Fred shouted, "Go, go, go!" But Joey, heart pounding, yelled, "Stop the car! He's hurt!" Steve, in full freak-out mode, slowed just enough for Joey to leap out, sliding on his hands and knees across the pavement before sprinting back to Larry's still form. I'd heard the crash from our house and was already out the door, Henry bounding beside me, his tortilla scent trailing like a weird cologne. By the time we reached them, Joey was kneeling over Larry, praying like his life depended on it: "Please, God, don't let him die! Put his injury on me but cure this man! Forgive me, Lord, I didn't mean

to hurt him—I was stupid and didn't think this through. I know you can perform miracles, please cure him!" Just then, Henry, never one to miss a dramatic moment, leaned in and gave Larry's face a slobbery lick that could've revived a coma patient.

Larry's eyes fluttered open, and he sat up, blinking like he'd just woken from a decade-long nap. "Young man, what am I doing here?" he asked, voice soft, almost tender. Joey, stunned, stammered, "You ran into our car!" Larry tilted his head, genuinely confused. "Why'd I do that?

Are you okay, young man?" The concern in his voice was so alien it gave me whiplash. This was the guy who'd screamed about government cheese at 3 AM, and now he sounded like Mr. Rogers after a yoga retreat.

I stood there, dumbfounded, as Larry refused an ambulance, insisting he was fine. "Come in for coffee," he said, gesturing to his house like he was hosting a book club. Inside, his wife, Ellen—a weary woman with a perm that hadn't changed since 1985—and their teenage daughter, Sarah, emerged, looking as baffled as we were. Larry hugged them, kissing their foreheads, but hesitated. "Uh, what're your names again?" he asked, like he'd misplaced his own family. Ellen shot me a look that screamed, *What in the actual hell?* I pointed at Joey, shrugging. "Kid prayed him well. That's all I got." The room smelled faintly of motor oil and regret, but Larry was all smiles, offering us instant coffee like we were old pals.

I drove Joey home, his knees scraped and his eyes glassy, like he'd seen the face of God in a station wagon windshield. We didn't talk much until I pulled up to his house, decked out in Christmas lights so bright NASA could've used them for navigation. Joey opened the door, then turned back, a shy grin breaking through. "I'm sure that when Jesus healed the crippled, he didn't leave them with a limp. I prayed that Jesus would heal Larry and it looks like he did" he said. "Merry Christmas, Mr. Warr." I nodded, feeling like I'd just walked through a Frank Capra movie. "Merry Christmas, kid."

Larry was never the same after that night. The Maryland Man, once a snarling tornado of conspiracy theories and flashlight swings, became... well, Sweet Larry. He stopped the midnight drag races, traded his rants for awkward small talk about the weather, and even started mowing his lawn (though the eggshells stayed). The neighborhood kids, robbed of their monster, lost interest, their egg-throwing crusades fizzling out. Casey retired his Larry Alarm, though he repurposed it to scare squirrels from Vickie's garden. Julie added a final chapter to her journal, titled "The Christmas Miracle of Maryland Street," and Vickie, ever the teacher, used the whole saga to lecture her students on empathy, redemption, and the dangers of egg-based warfare.

Three years later, we got an invite to a backyard BBQ at Larry's, where he grilled burgers. Joey was there, arm around Sarah, Larry's daughter, who was now his fiancée. The two had bonded over shared apologies and a mutual love of cheesy rom-coms, their romance blooming like a

weed in Larry's once-barren yard. Larry raised a glass of lemonade (he'd sworn off anything stronger), toasting, "To neighbors, second chances, and not hitting cars with flashlights!" We laughed, Henry wagged his tortilla-scented tail, and even Peewee, perched on the fence, gave a smug purr of approval.

Albuquerque wasn't Cloudcroft, but it had its own magic. That underpriced house and new friends. Best deal we ever got. And as for Crazy Larry, the Maryland Man? He was proof that sometimes, all it takes is a slippery egg, a kid's prayer, and a dog's slobber to turn a villain into a friend.

Happy Christmas by Todd Brady de Garcia

Who ever heard of something, or someone, as silly-ridiculous as a Christmas moth? Of course no one has, at least not about Christmas specifically, because moths are already everywhere, all the time, not only during Christmas. Since it's highly unlikely that anyone who is currently reading or hearing this story ever knew, or would ever know, that Once Upon a Time there was a Christmas moth, it's long past time for that to happen for you. So, keep on reading or listening and you'll see, starting with the question 'what would a Christmas moth's name even be?' Even saying the words 'Christmas moth' too many times in a row, or too quickly is like trying to whistle with a mouthful of mashed potatoes, so, having an actual name to say, in place of trying to say what he was most famous for, would be a very helpful beginning.

Happenstance, if you must know; also goes by Happy for short, and for sounding a little bit less pretentious. Yep, Happenstance, or Happy as we'll call him more familiarly, because familiarity and family are kind of 'related' in a

17

way. We'll be able to see each other as being a family with him pretty quickly, you'll see, that is, if we would be able to see him at all, even if he was sitting absolutely still, right in front of us both; blending right into whatever he was right next to like a true champ; also, like practically any other moth would do.

Kind of a weird irony (something you'd be surprised that moths are able to see and understand; little known fact) that although our friend's nickname is Happy, he really wasn't; in fact, he hardly ever was, if you want to be completely truthful about it. He could fly around just fine, ate stuff, could get a good day's sleep, made friends sometimes, at least for a little while, and certainly wasn't opposed to that ever happening whenever it didn't or did. Still, he was definitely way more Happenstance than Happy.

Happy-if-and-when-it-ever-happens is more like it. Happy is just way easier to say, so he just went along with it anyway and, over time, as you would expect, it became a thing that all of the other moths would automatically attach with his name; without him ever really matching that, in moodiness. Imagine living long enough to become some sad-sack middle-aged moth who was still stuck, after all of these moth-years, with only ever being known as "Happy." Pretty quickly, you'd see how that could lead to some sorta-severe, moth-level social awkwardness; something that eventually became easier to just avoid altogether.

Don't worry. He didn't fly around all sad and stuff all the time. Other moths would just think a certain thing when they'd hear that his name was "Happy", and then, when he wasn't like that after all, well… you know; awkward-silent-moth eye-blinks while quickly computing any other avenues of mutual interest in order to remain at all conversant with each other. Kinda sucked, at least sometimes. If an eavesdropping moth could make a great big fake "boohoo" about something, and then immediately laugh about it, there's the cue.

You may ask, what's the big deal anyway? What could a moth possibly need so much that, when they don't get it, it would bring them unhappiness so predictably? Listen to the laughter of some of the neighborhood butterfly beauties when a moth flies by, especially a moth that looks as ordinary as Happenstance, and then you'll know what's up with what. As petty as it may sound to anyone else, to a moth, seeing a spectacularly beautiful butterfly laughing out loud about your imagined possibilities of reaching even any-level of sub-pretty, one that you'd obviously never be able to achieve; well, that can be pretty demoralizing (another experience that most don't realize a moth could ever know anything about; now you do.)

At about the same time that Happenstance had finally had enough of not being the right-kind-of-Happy, and enough of the never-gonna-be-nearly-pretty-enough to be mistaken for ever being even someone else's discarded butterfly, no matter how drunk on milkweed nectar the neighborhood butterflies ever got, even for the nice ones who at least wouldn't be laughing about it; he quietly just flitted away the way that moths usually do.

The thing about stuff that is obvious, is that whatever it is, it wasn't always obvious. There's always that one, discovering-it-time for the first time, on behalf of everybody else, even for the now-obvious stuff. As he was flying away from moth-town, our good friend Happenstance was just about to become one of those happens-once-then-someday-become-obvious ones. He'd have been happy to tell you that story before eventually dying of old age; truly Happy at the end of the day.

It was all because of that Great-Big-Solid-Bright-Star; unmoving, night after night after

night. Happenstance had become transfixed by it
one night, while all the other moths were busy
doing their own busy stuff. After a few nights of
staring at it all night long, he'd find himself
waking up again, right at dusk, and that Great
Big Star would be the first thing that he'd look
for; always right there, all big and bright, lodged
way up high in the sky in that exact spot where it
had been through the whole night before.
Without saying anything to anyone else, because
nobody would understand why he'd become
transfixed by it anyway, and any delay for any
explanations would only become greatly
annoying and make everything even more
confusing to everyone; he took off from moth-
town to find out what was up with that Great-
Big-Star. A star so solid-bright he couldn't think
of anything but getting closer to it; as close to it
as he could possibly get, no matter how far away
it still was. And, while nobody was looking,
there he went.

With no way of measuring what time-or-distance
is for a moth, Happenstance would never be able
to tell anyone how long it took for him to get
there, or how many rest stops in the middle of
nowhere he'd had to take. His wings though, he
would love to tell you about those. You'd think
that by going an immeasurable distance, through
innumerable, navigationally precarious potential

for missteps, he would have arrived at that star practically disassembled as a moth, mentally, physically, and in spirit, due to the exhaustion alone. But, in fact; no. The closer that he got to that Great-Big-Bright-Star the stronger and the more determined he felt about getting there. That seed of a feeling that had started somewhere within him, back in moth-town, right from the first time that he saw that Great-Big-Star, grew within him like it was its very own turbo-engine power-source; created in a moth-version, of course.

By the time that he got to where that Great-Big-Star had led him, a shamble-barn that immediately felt as home-sweet-home as any place on earth possibly could, ever, his whole moth body spirit and soul were all overflowing with purpose, like some invisible incandescence, even though he'd never have been able to tell you what that purpose was to be, for him. At least not quite yet.

He quietly glided right-up and landed perfectly, right onto the lip of a very old cradle where he saw a brand new cutie-cute human-looking baby, who, even though most human babies are at least a little bit cute, this one seemed to bring everyone else who had gathered there, all at the same time as Happenstance, to be standing there all mesmerized by that exceptional cutie-cuteness of that baby. Each of them had been brought to that same spot on the planet, with the same unwavering focus and unrelenting drive that had brought him there, and, even with all the multitudes who had gathered, of every type, and from every corner of everywhere… there was quiet.

Happenstance looked at the baby, as quiet as a moth can be, when a thought or a feeling passed through his mind and his soul in a way that told him, distinctly, that this was not just another one of his internal dialogues that was about to happen. Somehow, this would be a conversation, with this same cutie-cute little baby who was looking directly at him.

"What's the big deal about getting all hung-up on not being as pretty as a butterfly, Happy? There's a whole lot more to stuff than that."

"Umm, I don't know how you know about that, but yeah, it kinda bugs me about why they all got all lucky like that, and I got left with having to reach for hopefully being at least ordinary, on my best days; although, none of that feels like it even matters anymore anyway, because being here with you, right now, is everything that will ever matter to me. And, by the way, for the very first time, coming from anybody, thank you for calling me Happy."

"I'm very glad to hear that, and thank you for that too, because here's the deal, Happy. I always lean-in towards those who don't jump-right-out with all of their beauty-and-purpose already in place, like it had all been pre-packaged that way. I love the less obviously beautiful, who, like you, usually go unseen. Have you ever looked closely at any moth's wings? At your own wings? They're completely fantastic, with an incredible beauty that you would find unimaginable until you stop and look closely enough. Not to be confused with beauty being your purpose; I just wanted to be sure that you noticed that. Your purpose in life, in being here with me today, will last for thousands of years; longer than any beauty I could have offered to you as a butterfly. I know that it's probably weird to hear my baby-Jesus-mind conversing with you like this, although, along with knowing a whole bunch about other stuff, knowing that you already know that I mean it literally, when I say that your purpose in being here will last for thousands of years. I'm glad to see that you find that fact puzzling, because that gives me an opportunity to explain it to you. See, it's like this: remember how you felt when you saw that great big star in the sky, turning out to be right above the place where I was born?"

"Yes, my dear cutie-cute baby Lord Jesus, it's like the light from that Big-Bright-Star was pulling me towards you with a level of magnetism that I had never known existed before. I knew, whatever it meant and whatever it took to do it, I was going to be here with you, exactly like this, exactly like I am right now. I knew that I had to be here, even before knowing what 'here' was, quite yet."

"That, my friend Happy, is exactly what will last for thousands of years because of you, because of the way that you listened, the way that you followed without even having to understand anything about why, quite yet; you just knew, and then, you just did what you knew to do."

"Yes sir, I did that." Happenstance said, through his waving antennae, to baby Jesus, and, without wanting to say it all-out-loud, all the way Happy.

"Because of what you have brought of yourself here, representing all moths from everywhere who will ever be, every moth will now be drawn towards light the same way that you have been drawn to me through my great big star. They won't know how to stop themselves from

25

wanting to be as close to the lights they find, as you have been with mine, on your way to being here with me today. So, from now until the time that we return together again, how-ever-many thousands of moth-years from now that turns out to be, every type and generation of moth being drawn towards light will be a reminder, to anyone who is observant about anything that's even remotely spiritually relevant (I know, big thoughts for a brand new cutie-baby; you see, I've got a whole lot to do in just 33 years, so I had a little bit of a head-start), this moment will be seen through multitudes of human beings observing moths for generations, everywhere; each one fluttering and flittering all around any light that they see, the very same way as you have here, coming all of this way to find me. This will be our reminder, for generations and generations, to follow the feeling of that Great-Big-Star, just like you did; right here. There could be no greater purpose than that, my Happy friend, and that is all yours; your sacred purpose. It did not require having your own set of brightly colored and, in my humble opinion, overtly attention-seeking wings. It just took you doing what you somehow already knew to do, finding me here today. Hopefully, that will help people begin to wonder, 'well, who was or is that cutie-baby-guy who had that Great-Big-Important-Star to begin with, and what's the rest of the story of what happened next; for forever."

"The forever part of forever, huh baby Jesus."

"Yep, the forever part of forever. Thanks for that, my Happy moth-friend."

"Thank you too my tiny, beautiful-baby-friend Jesus. Thank you."

Now, my dear reader or listener of this Happy Christmas story, when you see a moth flying all around that bright light at your front porch at night, you'll know why that moth is doing all of that flying, right there; reminding you, for the moment that you take to remember important stuff. And, while you're still inside of that moment you can say, right out loud, "thanks, Happenstance." Or, if you choose to, you can just say "thanks, Happy" …because now, we're family too.

happy
The moth

Popcorn Balls and Snowflakes by Anna Jean Seibert

The smell of popcorn cooking recently took me back to a very fun memory. I want to share with someone, I guess you are that someone.

I was a busy mother of three active young girls. It was early December, and I was already feeling the pressure of all the activities and responsibilities of Christmas. You know, it is one of my favorite times of the year, but cookies to bake, everyone's Christmas parties to keep up with (my December calendar looked like it had a skin disease). Did I have enough gifts for my girls, did I remember gifts for all our large extended family. I was stressed!

So, I baked cookies. I thought of all the people I wanted to give some to. I thought of all the children's parties that I had promised cookies to. And I got started on my cookie marathon.

I had in mind my next-door neighbor she had lost her husband that summer after a lingering illness. We would definitely take her some cookies. When we had delivered the cookies to her, one of my daughters said to me, "Miss Smith didn't have any Christmas decorations up in her house none at all"

Since our neighborhood decorated all fall and winter this was odd enough to make her wonder why.

"Her husband died last August. I think she must be too sad to want to celebrate and decorate." Sherrie was my eldest and only a little past five, the other two girls were even younger. I didn't want to try to explain any further.

I began to get our dinner started, and the girls all went back to play in Sharrie's room. I could hear them laughing and talking and no fights seemed to be brewing so I had no reason to go back and see what they were doing. I didn't object when they all trooped by going out to our backyard.

The next morning, early, I heard my front doorbell ring. "Who comes visiting at this time of the day." I wondered? I looked to see that it was my good neighbor carrying a covered tray. "What a surprise. Is everything OK?" I asked as I opened the door.

"Yes, I guess it is a surprise to you and to me both. Are your girls up?"

"Sure they are watching Saturday morning cartoons. What have they done? I was a little worried."

"Come and see she said." We went across our adjoining backyards to her back patio door. There, on the glass sliding door were dozens of white snowflakes cut from tablet paper and taped, only about three foot high, on her patio door.

"Your precious children
have given me back Christmas. I was reminded of when my own children were young, and we made popcorn balls and decorated them as ornaments for our Christmas tree. I got busy last night and made popcorn balls last night. I want to give each of your daughters one for your tree.".

"OH let's go and let you give them to the girls. I am wanting to see them, myself."

So, we walked back, and she gave each of them the most beautifully decorated popcorn balls I have ever seen, more elaborate than I could have done myself.

Later, I asked Sherrie how she and Angelique had learned to cut snowflakes. I knew I had never shown them. I was assured that 'no' they had not let the two-year-old use scissors.

"Our father showed us one time and I remembered it. I thought she needed decorations to make her happy."

"I think it worked."

Spirit of Christmas by Raymond Walter Seibert

"You're a thief," the voice on the phone accused me. "You know that property is worth twice what you are offering."

"Yes sir," I responded with as much calm as I could muster. This had been going on through agents for nine months and had come to a head with this phone call from out of the blue by the owner. "I know the property is worth what you are asking but what I am offering is all the money that myself, my wife and my father have in the world. The property will not finance, and I will not go in debt for it. The offer is 'take it or leave it'.

There was a long pause and a heavy blow and he said, "I'm going to sell it to you, but you stole it."

"I also have to have access, and it has to be platted."

"I'm not going to give you fifty feet so you can build a street and develop back there."

"I must have an 'ingress-egress' and it must be stated commercial."

That is how Jeanne and I came into possession of three point two-four acres of commercial property grandfathered residential. It was on the north-west corner of Beltline Road and Interstate Thirty-Five East. Ten Mile Creek was very near and the property between was flood plain as well as about half my acreage. Walking the property with my father, I excitedly stated, "I'll get a fortune for this property someday. I was in the Southland Life building years ago when it was still the tallest building in Dallas, and a model of the future city was on display. There was a twenty-story building sitting on this property. It's the closest buildable land to the Ten Mile Creek."

"No, you won't." my father said, shaking his head from side to side. "Two reasons why. First, they don't give that kind of money to guys like you. Two, when they get ready for this property, they will take it from you."

"Oh, Dad." I retorted, ignoring the slight in his estimation of my prospects, "that's so cynical."

He gave me a sideways squint of a wise look. "That's because you don't know what the hell is going on."

And so a few days before Christmas my family and myself moved into the solid brick house behind the Skating rink. The rink had the front onto Beltline Road with a parking lot that bordered on the front of my land. The back wall of the skating rink was about fifteen feet from my front porch, and the house would bounce to their music. When we moved in they were playing, "I Want A Brick House, Huhuu, Yeowow", and I loved it. We went out back on the property and cut a small cedar for our Christmas Tree.

I used the property and the barn to run my air conditioning contracting company. It was a one-horse operation, me. Still piles of condenser coils mounded each year in the back pasture, and some small commercial sales happened.

Many years passed and some springs we would sell small amounts of vegetables that grew in the garden in the front part of the property. The children grew up so fast, and soon we went to East Texas University to visit the youngest. East Texas is lush with timber and produce.

Greenhouses in towns along the way were numerous. Signs saying "Christmas Tree Farm" appeared along the highway, advising directions and milage to the farm. "Let's go look at some trees," I suggested to Jeanne. She didn't object and we turned off and went down a dirt road to the farm.

We had a pleasant walk along well-manicured pathways among live growing Christmas pine. The smell was intoxicating, and the weather was perfect that day. I went back to the office and requested a price sheet for wholesale sales.

"You can select your trees," I was assured. "Just bring your sales tax number."

It all seemed simple and now I 'had the bit between my teeth'. "What are you doing," Jeanne asked suspiciously? I turned in on a nearby farm with greenhouses.

"I just thought I might as well look in on the price of poinsettias," I said innocently. She gave me a worried look as to knowing my habit of 'buying for the shop' when we were traveling had created quite an accumulation of things, which we now hoped to sell in the Christmas rush. Her fears were well founded as I made a deal with the owner to come back and purchase one hundred poinsettias wholesale on November twenty-second, about three weeks in the future. It was a sum of money and Jeanne was not happy. Since she knew that I would be 'out on a service call', and she would be sitting at the Christmas shop in the afternoons after teaching that day and all-day Saturdays.

I also purchased two beautiful poinsettias for us and for the hostess of a Christmas party we were attending in a few days. This party had doctors and lawyers and city leaders attending. A Sunday Bible study group where I felt a need to share. A vanity or a Christmas spirit, I knew the beautiful Christmas flowers would be welcomed, and the hostess was moved to joyful tears at the gift.

I had recently acquired a small kiln and had a wonderful greenware shop in the neighboring town. In that neighborhood, I would stop in and browse the aisles of greenware stacked to the ceiling on shelves that lined the shop. I had discovered some small bells and angels along with candy cane and stars. These I bought and drilled a hole to hang as ornaments on Christmas trees. Bisk fired to a hardness and then glazed all white and fired again. Next, I took a very smelly and toxic solution and carefully placed the gooey substance around the bottom edge of the bells and on the angels' wings. Back into the kiln for a serious heating to red hot again. The bells emerged with a shiny gold rim, and the angels' wings were now golden.

I made these as presents to all my friends at the party. The air was electric with laughter and good spirits that evening. We could see our breath as we went caroling a few doors away at a friend's house who was recovering from a deadly accident. He had been injured in a foreign country doing charity surgery when a nick in a glove left him with a life-threatening blood disease. His recovery and survival was credited with prayer and was regarded as a miracle. He waved to our chorus from his dining room table. It was a Norman Rockwell picture of Christmas. I don't remember a better party.

The days moved along toward Christmas and knowing that I would make two trips, checked the weather and with no rain and little wind, set out to get the Christmas trees. When I arrived at the tree farm, frantic activity was taking place as trucks and trailers were being loaded continuously through the main yard. I went in and found a place to park and placed my order with the desk. I was directed to a spot in line and told to wait my turn. This was all business and nothing friendly going on. Eventually, it was my turn to load out.

"Now I was told that I could select my trees," I told the foreman who seemed to be in control.

He examined my order, "you got two eight-footers, one seven and twenty-two sixes. It's takem-as-they-come." That was it and he directed the truck and camper loaded with as many as he could stuff in. Then they loaded the trailer, but all the trees got turned into the wind instead of butt ending toward the wind, all the foliage was forward and would be catching the wind. I would be lucky to not have trees blow out of the trailer. Little did I know that my Christmas commercial anxiety had just begun.

Back at home, I stacked the trees against the front fence and parked the trailer. That weekend we sold the three big trees. "Things are looking good," I told Jeanne. "It was the expensive trees I worried about." Then the supermarkets got their trees in and placed them in front of the stores. There were Christmas trees everywhere I looked, and a week went by without another sale.

The pickup date for the poinsettias was approaching, and I was watching the weather. Late November and a Texas Blue Norther was being predicted for the very day of the pickup of the flowers.

The day started off warm for a November morning as I headed out. The poinsettias were perfect and wrapped to stand them up. The weather began to change as we were loading flowers. I had overestimated my capacity, and I soon had poinsettias in the floorboard, the front seat, and in the small area behind the seats.

Packed into the back pickup bed under the camper as tight as they would fit, I managed to stuff them all in and headed out for home.

The wind was strong out of the north and the temperature was changing rapidly. Soon, I needed heat in the cabin, and anxiety concerning the flowers in the camper began to grow. By the time that I reached the shop and started to unload, Dallas was getting a full-blown norther howling wind tried to rip each pot of poinsettias from my hand as I struggled to protect them and get them inside the shop. The propane wall furnace was warming the room. The old heating system had a pilot generator that furnished electricity to the thermostat and gas valve. It had been known to blow out in a strong wind and need to be relit. A new anxiety began to grip, and I checked the wall heater, and it felt good after facing the coming cold wind. We managed to get the poinsettias into a back room for storage, and all seemed good. Jeanne had sold a couple of trees and Christmas shopping was beginning.

It was about midnight, and a cold wind was blowing in great gusts. I got worried about the heater and dressed and went next door to the shop to check. My blood ran cold as I opened

41

the door and realized the shop was way too cold. Checking the wall furnace, the pilot light had blown out at some point earlier, how much earlier I couldn't tell, I relit the pilot and started the wall furnace again. Were the poinsettias damaged? It was not possible to know. But I did know. It was not possible that the flowers had not been stressed.

Over the next few days and weeks, we sold to friends and people that came into the shop. We had one large sale arranged with a very nice retail plant store. I held my breath as the owner of the plant store came to examine the flowers. She realized the weather had suddenly plunged in temperature and she was suspicious that the poinsettias would droop. I made the sale but did not feel good about it. The beautiful picture of all those flowers in Christmas colors was delightful. Now, my spirit was troubled.

The Christmas rush became a frantic parade. The Saturday of December twelfth I came in from a heating job. "We have grossed half a year of sales today," Jeanne proudly stated.

"Did we sell any of the Christmas trees?" I asked? The trees were selling very slowly, and

I did not want to be left with trees after Christmas.

"We sold one," she told me.

Sales slowed after the rush, and the weather turned colder. Poinsettias don't last. They are a frelicant plant, and the least stress will damage their beauty. We continued to run the shop, and a tree sold now and then until on Christmas morning there was only one left.

It was very early Christmas morning while we were eating breakfast, when a car pulled up in front of the remaining tree. "I guess I'll go out and sell this last tree," I said getting up and putting on my coat. It was cold out and I could see my breath fogging as I walked toward the man standing by his car. I had decided that I would give this tree away. It was the rejected tree after all, of small value.

"Is this tree for sale?" The man seriously asked me.

I picked the tree up and turned it around to show him. "This here 'Charlie Brown' tree is a good tree if you stand it in a corner where the bald spots don't show. "I'm making you a

Christmas present of this tree," I Tumped it on its butt end.

"I can pay for this tree," he seemed not to understand my magnanimous gesture.

"You can't pay for this tree," I laughed. "It's free."

He still seemed confused. I want to buy this tree for my daughter. I've been all over town looking for a Christmas tree, but everyone is closed. "You see," he continued in a halting manner. "We've been at the hospital with her mother. She was ill, and she died last night. I can buy this tree," he again insisted.

"You cannot buy this tree. It is free." I handed him the tree. He took it without another word and turned and stuffed it into the trunk of his car, where the bald spot made a tight fit but still stuck out so the trunk lid wouldn't close. The words 'Merry Christmas' stuck in my throat.

As I watched him drive slowly away toward Beltline Road and turn toward his home, tears were streaming down my face, and it began to sleet.

If Lost, You Will Be Found by Gina Lilly Carmichael

I want to tell you a story. It's a real Christmas story that happened on Christmas day 10 years ago and to those of us in the midst of it, it will live in our hearts forever.

Every story needs a setting, and this one is set in a small hill town in Massachusetts, my hometown. It's a beautiful little town of just over 1000 people. It has a town center with 2 churches, a town hall, one gas station, a hardware store, a post office and three cozy little restaurants all centered around a small lake. The freezing weather begins around Thanksgiving and rarely quits until Easter and that Christmas week, the frozen lake was full with hockey games at one end and ice fishermen out in the whistling wind at the other in spite of temperatures in the teens and wind chills lower still.

Most people assume Massachusetts is nothing but cities like Boston but out in Western Mass, in the Berkshire Mountains, it's still wild and wooded. You can drive for miles through the woods from one town to the next and only see the occasional house. There are no sidewalks or breakdown lanes, only roads cut into the woods with just enough room for a snowplow to do its work. Like I said, it's still on the wild side of geography.

Every year my cousin Sue and her better half Todd host the family party on Christmas day starting around one in the afternoon with enough food and merriment to keep the fun going late into the night. Sue makes her famous Norwegian Glogg and Cousin Jay entertains everyone with his professional magic act. The party draws family home from California, Texas, New York or wherever their lives and livelihood has taken them. The huge old Victorian home was once our grandparents before Sue and Todd and it feels like the beating heart of our family whenever it fills with loved ones of every age and generation.

Christmas morning dawned shiny and bright this year with a cover of fresh snow from the day before. A Rockwell-lovely scene to be sure, but windy and bitterly cold. The party got going as planned and was in fine fettle by five as the sun started to fade into dark. By six, it was, as my uncle Norm would say, "dark as a pocket." Everyone coming in from the cold felt a wonderful wave of heat enveloping them as they joined the warmth of 50-plus people and a kitchen full of simmering soups. With a 12-foot

Christmas tree in the front room and every light in the house on, it was a beautiful, shining sight.

Even though this home is on Main Street and the front door has its annual Christmas wreath, no one ever enters there. The path is not cleared, and the snow is deep from sliding off the slate roof above. The sweeping driveway wraps around the back, and everyone simply drives around and comes in the back.

At just after six, my niece Heidi was in the front room on the phone with brother Richard in New York who had to miss the festivities this year. She told him she thought she heard someone knocking at the front door, but it didn't make sense… as I said, no one ever uses it. She peeked out the window and saw an old man there and a dog. She was unsure at first what to do but Richard laughingly said, "It might be Santa, open the door!"

Heidi got the door open only to find a small stooped white-haired gentleman and an equally aged golden retriever with nearly as much white hair as her owner. The man was dressed in only a summer-weight jacket with no hat or gloves,

47

unthinkable for the freezing wind and weather. He asked for directions to Nash Hill Road. It didn't make sense. Nash Hill Road was in a town 15 miles away over rough country roads. He was very quiet and looked every bit like the Christmas Angel, Clarence in "It's a Wonderful Life."

Todd & Sue were found in the crowd, and they brought him and his dog inside out of the weather. They made their way to the kitchen to get him some warm soup and water for the dog. The poor dog could hardly walk. In the middle of the crowd, his quiet story slowly came together. He just wanted to stand quietly with his dog and not be a bother to anyone.

With his head bowed, standing in the kitchen amongst strangers, he slowly answered questions, piecing together very disoriented fragments of his day. He seemed so lost mentally, trying desperately to make sense of it all.

He and his wife had traveled from Connecticut to Massachusetts to visit her family for the day. At noon, he took their dog out for a short walk but got turned around on the country road and couldn't find his way back. He and the dog had been walking for six long hours through the wooded country roads, with no hat, gloves or boots in dangerous temperatures nearing zero. The horror of the story slowly started to sink in and the miracle that he survived had us all numb in disbelief.

A call was made to the state police, and they knew immediately who our guest was. They had been searching for him with dogs and a helicopter for nearly six hours and by now had feared the worst. In thirty minutes, a cruiser flew into the driveway, blue lights flashing, and a trooper came to bring him and his dog back to his family. Though the man tugged at her leash, the dog was unable or unwilling to leave the warm kitchen. My brother Steve scooped her up and carried her out to the waiting cruiser. By now everyone was crowded in the kitchen and as the cruiser pulled out of the driveway, Patrick exclaimed, "It's a Christmas Miracle!"

We all laughed, but felt warmed at being able to help, as we pondered the many ways our Christmas Miracle might not have been, and all the miracles of his day came to us…. The why's and what if's… What if he'd tripped along the cliffs of Chapel Falls and fallen off the road? What if he'd stopped to rest and not kept going?

What if a car had hit him in the dark, or hadn't had the courage to knock on a stranger's door? What if his family never found him again?

It was all so heart-wrenching and yet ended with such relief. We finally learned his name but, in my heart, he will always be Clarence, our Christmas Angel and I'll celebrate his courage every Christmas I live.

We all need to be brave in our lives and not let fear win out. The many little fears that keep us where we are in our lives and hold us back from something better. The fear of asking for help, the fear of trying something different and new, that won't let us open that door to the unknown. The bible has the phrase "Do not be afraid" 365 times. I like that, one for every day of the year.

So, raise a glass this year and toast to Clarence and pray for strength in all that you do in this year and the next…

Holy Night by Lee Hardesty

The house felt nicely warm as they came inside, hanging their coats up by the door.

He looked at his wife with concern. "Let's get you sitting down."

She smiled. "My feet are killing me." He helped her over to the couch and began to take off her boots. The lights from the Christmas tree lit her face in a soft glow as he massaged her swollen feet. "That's nice. I knew there was a reason I married you." She looked at him fondly over her swollen stomach.

"You know, we didn't have to go out tonight." As he massaged her legs.

"I like going to Mass. My family always went on Christmas Eve. Father gave a nice sermon tonight. Mmmm, harder, right there."

He diligently worked on her left calf. "I just don't get it. I never understood the story. He was a preacher, and his teaching changed the world. If he'd gotten his ass out of town when he heard the Romans were coming he could have kept teaching for the rest of his life."

His wife's laughter made him smile. She looked down at him lovingly. "God gave us his only son, and his willingness to die for us redeemed mankind. He gave up his life and died for our sins. There are some things more important then ourselves." She smiled as she unconsciously ran a hand over her swollen stomach. "One day you are going to understand that… Dad."

"I can't believe this will be our last Christmas alone together. Next year, Santa Claus will have presents stacked up under the tree. We'll have another stocking hanging from the fireplace, and a baby crawling around on the floor."

She laughed again. "She'll be walking by then, a toddler. If it's a girl." She said with a mischievous smile. "Boys are slower. Haven't you read any of the books I bought you?"

"I've been focused on other things. You know, painting the room and putting the crib together. We have to be ready."

That elicited a snort. "Yes, I remember the crib. How long did it take you to assemble it? Why did you have to modify it again?"

"They didn't fit right! It's not my fault that they sent us the wrong pieces!"

"It went together just fine after I read you the instructions."

He came up and sat beside her on the couch.

She leaned into him, her head resting on his shoulder as his arm slid around her. "Can you believe we are going to be parents? I can't wait to get this little bugger out of me so I can have my body back. I don't even remember what my own feet look like."

He looked down into her emerald-green eyes. "They're beautiful, just as they always were. Come on, let's get you to bed. Santa Claus can't come till you go to sleep."

* * *

The room was dark with only the glow of the bedside clock. He looked around, trying to understand what was wrong. That was when he heard a moan of pain from beside him. Fumbling for the lamp, its warm glow filled the room. His wife was sweating beside him, her face squinched up in pain.

"What's wrong! Are you OK?"

"I think I'm fine; in fact, I think I'm going to get my wish tonight."

He looked at her in panic. "But it's too soon! The doctor said it wouldn't be for another three weeks! I haven't finished the room yet!"

"Well, someone's decided that it's time. You should probable get the bag. And help me dress." His wife started doing that panting-breathing thing they had practiced in class.

The walk was a struggle, as he tried to carry the bag in one hand as he helped her down the steps to the car. The seat belt barely fit around her as he fastened his wife into the car.

It was slippery; the snow was heavy, having fallen all night. He had to go inside for a pitcher of water to pour over the windshield to clear the ice.

There were only a few cars on the road braving the weather. Maybe if he had better tires, he might have been able to stay on the road when the approaching truck slid out of its lane. They weren't going that fast, but nothing happened as he slammed on the brakes. The last thing he remembered was the tree.

The smell was strong and acrid as he tried to push away the airbag. He heard a whimper of pain beside him as he desperately pushed the hot bag out of the way to see his wife. Her face was ghostly white, a rictus of pain.

"Are you all right?" His wife didn't answer. She couldn't answer. She barely seemed to be able to breathe through the pain. Looking down, the seat was wet with blood. "Oh, God! Hang on! I'll get help! Just hang on!"

The door had crumpled along with the front of the car. He had to kick it to get it open. "Nine one one. What is your emergency?"

"We crashed our car! My wife is having a baby! Something is wrong! She's hurt! You have to help us!"

"Try to calm down, sir. What is your location?"

He tried to breathe. "We're on 1431 east of Jonestown. We went off the road and hit a tree. She's hurt. There is blood everywhere. Something is wrong. We need help!"

"Stand by, sir. The roads are not clear. We have limited resources available. Stay on the line with me. Can you give me your full name and date of birth?"

There was a car coming. He could see the headlights through the snow. He hung up the phone as he struggled up the bank to the edge of the road, waving frantically as the car sped by. "Stop!" The night was dark as the taillights disappeared into the falling snow. The one remaining headlight from the car below formed a solitary pool of light in what felt like a sea of darkness.

Another set of headlights were coming closer, this time the other way, from town. Another large truck, like the one that had run them off the road. Waving his arms, he screamed as he stumbled towards it. The truck's horn blared, dropping in pitch as it rushed past, almost hitting him. He watched through his tears as its lights disappeared into the distance.

A cry echoed up to him from below, and he rushed back to the car. His wife was hunched forward, her arms wrapped around her belly, hands covered in blood. Her face was a mask of pain, and she was unable to look up as he called her name. "Listen to me. You have to hang on. Help is coming. You're going to be OK!"

Please, God, help us. Don't let her die.

That was when he heard a voice from behind him. "You folks OK down there?"

Looking up the hill towards the road, he saw a man leaning out the window of a van. Strains of big band jazz drifted down to him from the open window. It felt like a lifeline being thrown to them. "Down here! She's hurt. My wife is hurt!"

Soon he was surrounded by three black men as they helped him lift his wife out of the car. The seat was soaked in blood. "We got to get you folks to tha mergency room, right now!" The largest picked her up as though she was as light as a feather as he carried her to the van. They laid her in the back seat as well as they could. He cradled his wife's head in his lap as the van lurched forward with the spinning of tires on the slick road.

"Just hang on, we're going to be at the hospital soon. We're almost there. Everything is going to be allright." As he stroked his wife's hair through a wave of pain.

"That's right. We almost there. Don't worry. Cass is the best wheelman around. He's from Chicago. This little bit of snow, this is nothing to him." As he nodded towards the small, wiry little man driving the car. "We come a long way tonight. Just glad we could be here to help."

She tried to focus on him if only as a distraction to the pain. "Thank you. Thank you so much. Who are you?"

"You can call me Mel. Little man up there is Cass. Not only is he the best driver, but he is also the best piano player west of the Mississippi. You already met Balthassar. He wont answer to nothin shorter." Pointing to the big man, who barely seemed to fit into the passenger seat. "He don't talk much, he the drummer. And I…" As he pointed proudly to his own chest, "play the trumpet."

"You're musicians?"

"Yes mam. We got a gig in town down on Sixth Street. Come all the way from Abilene tonight. We're a jazz trio." Motioning to the equipment that filled the back of the van.

"That's nice. I like jazz." Her eyes closed again as her face contracted in another wave of pain.

As they crossed under one eighty three A he could see the lights of the hospital off to their left. There was a large nativity scene on an island in the parking lot in front of the hospital. As the van pulled up to the emergency entrance, Christmas music could be heard playing from the speakers under the porte-cochere.

"Help! We need help!"

People came running as Balthassar carried her through the doors of the emergency room. What followed seemed like an endless series of questions. People were shouting things he couldn't understand as they swarmed around her.

"The amniotic sac is ruptured. I've got a lot of bleeding."

"Blood pressure is dropping. We need an IV!"

"Ultrasound shows a placental abruption. I see a lot of bleeding. We need to go in!"

The nurse was trying to keep him calm. "Mr Conrad, I need you to listen to me. Your wife needs emergency surgery. We need to stop the bleeding. You have to make a decision. It may not be possible to save them both. We need your permission to terminate the fetus if we have to choose." She was trying to talk softly but there was so much going on in the room that her voice carried.

"No! No! You save my baby!" She was reaching up clinging to the doctor's jacket as they tried to put the IV in.

"Ms Conrad, we can't control the bleeding; we may have to perform an emergency hysterectomy. If we try to save both of you, you could…"

"I don't care! Whatever it…" Another wave of pain washed over her. "My baby! I chose my baby!"

"That's it! We need to move her! Prep the OR!"

"No! You can't! You have to save my wife! I forbid it!" The nurse was trying to restrain him as they rushed his wife out of the bay.

"It's her choice. They will do their best. Orderly! Can I get some help here!" And then a large man was pulling him out of the room as he watched his wife being rushed down the hallway, disappearing among a crowd of doctors and nurses.

* * *

The glass of the observation bay was thick and soundproof. Only a low thumping sound could be heard inside when he beat on it. The movement inside the room was frantic. They could not hear him scream. They did not have time to look up to see the tears that he wept as he leaned against the glass that separated him from his wife. He did not even notice as the nurse rushed out of the room with the infant. His eyes were fixated on his wife. And when they removed the tube from her throat and covered her face with the sheet, her pain was finally over and she seemed to be at peace.

Mel held him as he wept, and he felt Balthassar's large hand silently on his shoulder as the little man, Cass, looked on.

* * *

His head hurt as he slumped in the chair. It was the headache you feel when there just aren't enough tears to wash away the pain. Mel and the other musicians sat in chairs around him, unable to ease his grief. Someone had brought him coffee as if that would help. He needed a drink. Hell, he needed the whole damn bottle. It seemed like only moments ago his life was perfect. He had everything. Now everything was gone.

Mel was talking. He wasn't sure how long he had been speaking. "I don't know why he chose to take her from you tonight. Sometimes things just don't make no sense. But you have to trust in him. That he has a plan for all things. And that all of this happened for a reason…"

He looked up through his red swollen eyes. "A reason? What reason could there ever be for this? My wife is dead!"

At that moment there was a knock on the door of the room. A pair of nurses stood in the doorway. "Mr Conrad? Joseph Conrad?" They came forward into the room. "We have your daughter." Only then did he notice the bundle she was carrying in her arms. They came forward and placed the infant in his arms. She seemed so small wrapped in the cloth of her blanket. All he could see was her pink face. At that moment, her eyes opened, and she lifted an arm to reach towards him. Extending a single finger towards her, she grasped it in a tiny hand. He marveled at the perfect little fingers grasping and holding on to his own.

"What are you going to call her? We need a name for the paperwork. Her mother… There wasn't time."

As he looked down into her green eyes, his daughter smiled up at him with a look of total trust and complete love that promised joy and laughter. The pain seemed to fade away as he looked down into her eyes. The eyes that he knew.

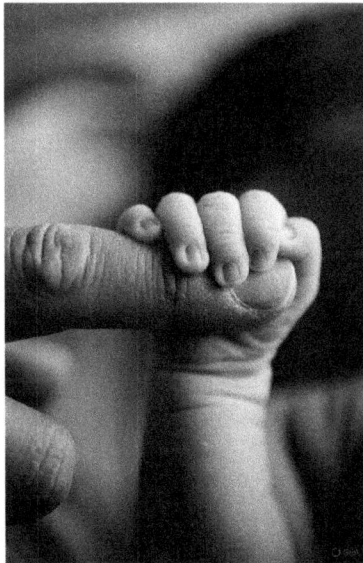

"Mary. Her name is Mary, like her mother."

The Flying Mattress Christmas by Derek Day

It was always Mema's favorite time of year. And
when Mema was happy, the
rest of us were bound to be happy too.

Mom had brought me and my sisters—Layla and
Missy—to the print shop, where
Mema and Grandpa John would be picking us
up.

They pulled up in John's 1987 red Subaru—his
pride and joy. (Years later
I'd learn to drive stick in that very car and go on
more adventures than
I'd ever admit to Mema.) Behind the Subaru was
a trailer stacked high with
brand new mattresses, still wrapped in plastic
like giant marshmallows.

We were headed to the lake house on Lake Leon,
a few hours east—a place
where summer memories clung to the dock and
winter always smelled like

pine and cocoa. This was our second Christmas
there, and we were going a
day early to help Mema and John get things
ready before the rest of the
family arrived.

☐

The Long Ride East
About fifteen minutes into the drive, Mema
asked, "John, are you sure
those mattresses are tied down good?"

He waved a hand and said, "They're fine,
sweetheart."

In the back seat, Layla had her Walkman on, lost
in Duran Duran. Missy had
Barbie and Ken debating which color sports car
they'd get married in. I
was in my own world, imagining Snake Eyes
ambushing Cobra Commander across
the console.

An hour later, Mema asked again if he was really
sure. John sighed and
fished some peppermint candy from his shirt
pocket—where his cigarettes
used to live—and turned up the radio to
Christmas music. "Everybody sing

along!" he said.

We did. For a while.

☐

Trouble on I-20
Two hours later, we were off the freeway and
onto the winding East Texas
backroads. Mema turned down the radio and
said, "John, I'm just asking one
last time—"

"Helen!" John interrupted, raising his voice just
enough to make the
Subaru tense up. "They're fine! It's all backroads
from here. And Derek,
quit bugging your sister."

He only called her "Helen" when he was truly
exasperated. Even Barbie and
G.I. Joe called a truce.

That's when Layla pointed out the window.
"Grandpa John! Look! Your
mattresses are flying!"

John slammed the brakes.

We watched through the rear window as two mattresses sailed gracefully
into a ditch like runaway parade floats. Without a word, John climbed out,
stomped through the weeds, and hauled them back one by one. His candy cane
fell out of his pocket halfway through the second one.

When he got back in the car, his face said everything. "Nobody say a word."

We didn't.

For about five minutes.

☐

The Flying Mattress Joke
Then little Missy piped up from the backseat, her voice all sugar and
sincerity:
"Mema, Grandpa John… I'll still act surprised if I get one of those flying
mattresses for Christmas."

There was silence.

Then John snorted. Then Mema giggled. Then the whole Subaru erupted in

laughter—except for Missy, who just looked
confused, trying to figure out
what was so funny about her very reasonable
Christmas wish.

John reached back and squeezed her leg
affectionately, tears of laughter
in his eyes. "You just might, sweetheart. You
just might."

☐

Christmas at Lake Leon
By the time we hit the dirt road to the lake house,
the world was dark
except for the glow of Christmas lights waiting
for us ahead.

Mema had gone full North Pole this year. The
yard was a winter wonderland
of Santa, reindeer, and twinkling lights reflecting
off the lake. Inside,
the house was bursting with Christmas magic—
the smell of cinnamon, the
crackle of the fireplace, and a tree so tall it
brushed the ceiling, with
the moonlight shining through the window
behind it.

Underneath it sat what looked like a hundred gifts.

Mema told us each to open one small present before bed. John dragged in
the mattresses—this time firmly grounded—and Mema dressed them in fresh
sheets and blankets.

Layla and Missy shared a room, and I had my own next door. We brushed our
teeth, whispered about Santa, and drifted off to the sound of frogs and
wind chimes.

☐

The Night Surprise
Sometime in the night, Missy woke everyone by shouting, "Mema! I don't
want a flying mattress! I wanna stay here!"

Mema came rushing in, laughing so hard she could barely talk. John
followed behind her, rubbing his eyes and shaking his head, muttering,
"Guess I'll keep an eye on that trailer in the morning."

Everyone went back to bed smiling.

Epilogue
Years later, every Christmas at Lake Leon,
someone would bring it up.

"Remember the Flying Mattress Christmas?"

John would grin, Mema would wink, and
Missy—now all grown up—would roll
her eyes and say, "I still never got that flying
mattress."

And John, without missing a beat, would smile
and say, "That's 'cause you
were already sleeping on one, sweetheart."

And we'd all laugh—just like that night in the
Subaru—because the best
Christmases aren't about perfect gifts or fancy
trips. They're about
Mema's joy, John's stubbornness, and the
laughter that still echoes down
those old East Texas backroads.

Rekindled Light by: Levi Day

He lies awake in his bed. His alarm is blaring, his tired eyes barely open. He groans as he slaps the alarm clock, feeling nowhere near prepared for the misery of the day.

I should be happy, this is a day of family and celebration.

But he doesn't believe in the holiday spirit at all. He hates the idea of Santa Claus. He hates the idea of Christmas. He hates the idea of spending money to make other people happy—mostly because he doesn't have any money to spend.

If he were a richer man, maybe he could. But every year, he sits there and looks into disappointed faces, unable to give anything more than a place to rest their heads and enough food to last them to the next day. Nothing more, nothing less. Not since she died.

It's just him taking care of his two boys.

How could anyone feel happy about Christmas in the face of such death and despair?

It's all a joke.

Christmas. Thanksgiving. Life.

What's the point? All I ever do is disappoint and disappoint and disappoint.

There is no point. I shouldn't be here.

I shouldn't be going through any of this. As a matter of fact… they'd probably be better off without me.

He reaches into his dresser.

He grabs a revolver and inspects it closely. The light glints off the shiny barrel.

Maybe this… this is the present they deserve. Getting rid of their rotten old man once and for all. Cut the bad fruit off the tree. Drop the dead weight so this plane can finally fly. This is what has to be done.

He places the barrel inside his mouth.

A single tear rolls down his cheek.

He shuts his eyes tightly as he squeezes the trigger.

Just then, he hears his boys yelling, "Oh my goodness, look at all these!" from the other side of the house—along with the sounds of the dog barking excitedly and running along with them.

His finger loses tension.

The hammer gently resets.

What are they yelling about?

He knows there isn't a single damn present in this house.

He sets the revolver back in the drawer and wipes the tear from his face—only for another one to follow.

He throws the blanket off and gets dressed: pants, shoes, shirt, hat. He rushes out the door, slamming it against the wall behind him as he shoots down the hallway.

As he gets close—

He feels it.

Happiness.

A feeling he hasn't felt since…

Since she was still here.

The light around the corner grows brighter and warmer.

This must be a dream.

When I turn that corner, it'll all be empty.

My kids… they're probably playing a joke on me. No shame on them—they're children.

I'll still smile. I'll laugh. I'll tell them it's okay. I'll start breakfast.

I'll hug them. I'll tell them I'm sorry for not being able to give them the Christmas they deserve.

Then suddenly, his youngest boy runs around the corner with a Viking helmet waving a toy sword around, yelling, "You won't take me!"

His oldest shouts back, "Arg, matey! You ain't going far! Pew pew pew!"

He turns the corner and sees his oldest one fully dressed in a pirate outfit, eyepatch and all, holding a playful blunderbuss-like toy. The dog is bouncing around behind him, wagging his tail, a bone bigger than he is clutched in his mouth.

"Kids… guys… come here. Where did y'all get these?" he asks sternly, assuming they stole them, grabbing the bone from his dog, who lets it go happily, tail still wagging.

"Dad, quit being silly. Are you trying to trick us?" his oldest says, firing a foam dart that bounces off his father's face—the dog tilts his head and smiles at the boy.

"You both will be grounded if you took these. Theft is not a joke."

"Dad… but aren't these for us?" His little one says, motioning toward the corner.

There it sits.

A magnificent Christmas tree.

The most extravagant, exquisitely decorated tree he has ever seen.

And underneath it, piles and heaps of presents, neatly wrapped, each with name tags hanging from them.

He walks over to the presents and kneels down, grabbing one of the smaller ones resting on top of the larger boxes. He inspects the name tag. It bears his son's name. Under "From," in elegant cursive writing, it reads:

Santa Claus.

Who did this? My brother? No. My aunt? Impossible. How could they have gotten in last night? I have cameras… a dog that barks… and two kids who wake up at anything…

However, he forces the questions aside so he doesn't ruin the moment for his children.

He stands, turns around, and hands the present to his little one, saying softly, "Merry Christmas."

"Thank you. I love you, Daddy," the little one says.

Later that evening, after putting his two beautiful boys to bed, he returns to his room and smiles—a long, genuine smile, so rare for him. He looks over at the empty side of the bed, and the smile fades.

At least my boys finally had a good Christmas again… "It's almost like you were here", he whispers.

The dog jumps onto the bed and curls up on the empty side, resting its head where she used to sleep.

He lies back beside the dog, petting it gently with one hand while picking up his phone with the other to check his messages.

Despite him telling them that they don't have to lie and that he just wants to thank them, his brother and his aunt both deny leaving anything in his house.

What in the world is going on? Are they really this committed to the bit? Maybe it isn't them…

He sets the phone on the nightstand, and as he does, he notices the dresser drawer is slightly open.

He definitely remembers closing it tightly this morning. He remembers this morning all too well, unfortunately.

He leans over and opens the drawer. The revolver is still in there, but lying on top of it is an envelope with his name on it.

He picks it up carefully.

It is sealed with a wax symbol in the shape of an "S."

He breaks the symbol as he opens it, and a scent drifts out.

Warm. Familiar. It's like Christmas.

But it wasn't like the cheap plastic scent of store-bought decorations; it was like the real thing—

A deep, comforting aroma of pine needles, a soft sweetness of cinnamon and nutmeg, and a warm, sugary whisper of fresh cookies pulled from the oven—

the kind that used to cling to her sweaters when she hugged him.

It smells like home.

It smells like the Christmas he thought he'd never feel again.

Inside the envelope, he pulls out a simple card, with white and silver flecks embroidered into it.

He opens it and sees a neatly handwritten note that reads:

"I hope this Christmas reminded you that even in your darkest hours, just one act of kindness can bring you back to the light."

— Santa Claus

www.ingramcontent.com/pod-product-compliance
Lightning Source LLC
LaVergne TN
LVHW050557090426
835512LV00008B/1214